Also by Avery Washington

Letters to My Daughters: Poetic Affirmations of Love from a Father

Legacy: 2nd Edition of Letters to My Daughters

Mother: A Heartfelt Poetic Tribute Celebrating Single Mothers

Just Speaking My Mind: Spoken Word Poetry Vol.1

A Love Letter to Our Beautiful Black Women

A Love Letter to Our Beautiful Black Women

Avery Washington

Happie Publishing
Katy, TX

Happie Publishing
Katy, TX 77494
inspiration@happiepublishing.com
832-422-8977 or 832-800-8962

A Love Letter to Our Beautiful Black Women

Copyright © 2019 by Avery Washington

All rights reserved. No part of this publication may be reproduced, stored in a retrieval system or transmitted in any form by any means, electronic, mechanical, photocopying, recording or otherwise without permission of the publisher.

ISBN - 13: 978-0-9990420-1-4
LCCN 2019900409

Dedication

This book is dedicated to my beautiful wife Kisha Washington.
Happy 20th wedding anniversary!
I love you!

"To you is where our hearts belong!"
Avery Washington

Contents

Dedication..ix

Preface..xvii

Acknowledgments..xix

Introduction..1

The Strength of Black Women....................................5

Thank You...8

So in Love...10

Heaven on Earth..11

Your Sweet Nectar...13

Queen..16

Superwoman..17

Heart and Soul..19

Supposed to Be...21

Stimulating Conversations......................................23

Say Her Name..25

Great Sacrifice...27

A Queen's Birthday...29

Her Love...32

King..33

If You Were Gone..35

The Love of You..37

Angel...38

The Rain...39

Look in My Eyes..41

My Responsibility...43

Tasty Love..45

The Proposal...46

A Deeper Connection..47

My Prayer..49

Loving You..51

Phone Sex 53

Over and Over 55

Hello 57

Still in Love 59

A Precious Jewel 61

Making Sweet Love 63

Your Smile 66

Our Love Will Be 67

Daily Motivation 69

Not a Trophy to Me 71

The Vowel Renewal 73

Preface

I'm a very proud black husband and father of three beautiful daughters and I was raised in a single parent home. Throughout my life I have always been surrounded by strong and beautiful black women, but as a youth I never thought about the impact that being around these great women would have on my life.

Most of my years as a toddler were spent with my mother and great-grandmother teaming up to raise me. My mother worked a lot to provide for me and she needed someone who she could depend on to be there for both of us. Big Momma is what we called my great-grandmother and I truly enjoyed all of the quality time that I spent with her. We would have long conversations as we walked to the bus stop while on our way to church on Sundays. Big Momma would also teach me how to cook hot water cornbread, mustard greens and many other great things that we would eat deep down south in New Orleans, Louisiana.

My mother also had sisters that would step in to watch me at times along with my grandmother and grandfather. I clearly remember taking trips with my grandfather collecting cans and exchanging them for cash at the recycling plants. He was a great man and I'm certain much of my character and hard work ethic stems from him.

At the age of twenty-six I fell in love and married a gorgeous woman. Ironically, she was a single parent and her birthday was one day after my mother's. God has blessed us with two more beautiful daughters within our marriage giving us a total of three. I would like to say during the year of this book's release that we are celebrating our twentieth year wedding anniversary.

My love for my beautiful daughters propelled me to write my bestseller *Letters to My Daughters*. I'm best known for writing this book and it continues to be a blessing to many families and has been a number one bestseller many times over. *Letters to My Daughters* has also afforded me the opportunity to advocate the significance of father and daughter relationships. In 2018, I was a featured author at the NAACP Annual Convention in San Antonio, TX. I also was a speaker at the 2018 Congressional Black Caucus in Washington, D.C.

I have consciously decided to dedicate my life to paying homage to our beautiful black queens, because they have made great sacrifice for the betterment and very existence of black men and we owe our lives to them.

My gift to you is to continue using my gift of writing to uplift, praise, encourage and show the immense respect that I have for you. I love you and I sincerely hope you enjoy *A Love Letter to Our Beautiful Black Women*.

Acknowledgments

I have to start by thanking my awesome wife Kisha of Cruise Planners. Thank you for believing in my dream and investing in me. You bought me my first laptop to start my writing career and I will never forget that. I will always love and appreciate you.

To Jalene Mack, Founder of Mack Performing Arts Collective. MPAC has always provided opportunities and platforms for networking and education throughout the Houston area. I thank you for the many doors you and your organization has opened for me and I will be forever thankful.

To La Trisha McIntosh and La Tasha Taylor of Beautifully Said Magazine. Thank you for featuring and supporting me early on in my writing career. We have stayed true to our visions of putting out positive content for our communities and beyond.

To Kris Green (KG Smooth), host of Access Houston on 97.9 The Box. I thank you sincerely good brother. Our conversation on your show was very powerful, informative and piercing to the hearts and ears of your listening audience as we discussed family advocacy and systemic racism in our communities. I look forward to having more intellectual conversations with you soon as we continue to fight to create positive change.

To Judy Foston Stanford of Foston International Communications Inc. I thank you for sharing your huge platform at MJWJ and allowing me to share the significance of father and daughter relationships with a very large listening audience. You provided me with my first radio station interview and it was at that point I knew God was using me to touch the lives of many.

To John Stanford of MJWJ. Thank you for having me as a guest on your radio show and for all the positive words of encouragement. I have great respect for you as a man and graduate of Tuskegee University.

To Evelyn Arrington of MJWJ. I thank you for having me as a guest on your radio show and I appreciate how you broke down my book *Letters to My Daughters* biblically. You truly added a much deeper meaning in our discussion for your listeners.

To Emilian V. White, President / CEO of Amazing 102.5 FM. I remember reaching out to you at an MPAC event and you not only gave me your word, but you made things happen for me and I appreciate you tremendously. Much respect to you.

To T. C. Thompkins of Music and Conversations. You are very tall in stature, but also when you give your word it stands tall. I was blessed to introduce myself to you at an MPAC event. You invited me to be on your nationally syndicated radio show immediately and I sincerely thank you for blessing me with that opportunity. I know we will work together again.

To Nettie Jones (The Girlfriend's Therapist). Thank you for having me as a guest on your great show. I wish you continued success in blessing many lives with your practice and I look forward to having more productive discussions with you to help with mental health in our communities.

To Mocha Ochoa Nana, CEO / Founder of The Oracle Group. Meeting you has truly been a blessing to me. You have provided many platforms for authors to share their work. I look forward to working with you again soon and wish many blessings upon you. I want to sincerely thank you for believing in my messaging of family advocacy.

To Velman Trayham, CEO / Founder of Thinkzilla Consulting Group. Thank you for believing in my vision and inviting me to speak as a panel guest at your *When God Says Go* book signing in Houston, TX. You have always been a genuine soul and I appreciate you always.

To Isiah Carey, Host of Isiah Factor Uncensored. I remember you supporting me early on by purchasing a few of my books and posting them on your social media sites. You have touched the lives of many people in the world by always speaking and bringing the truth. I thank you.

To Karen Jackson, Founder / CEO of Sisters Network Inc. I appreciate all of the encouraging words and support you have given me throughout the years. I have only met you once, but I pay close attention to those who genuinely encourage me and spread positive energy. I appreciate you more than you know.

To Hilton J. LaSalle Ed.D., Founder of LaSalle Consultants. Thank you for the advice and great suggestions of books to read. I enjoyed working with you in the past and continue to look forward to us working together on future projects.

To Liz (Zoe) Anderson, host of In Your Favor Radio Show. Thank you for sharing your great platform and your listening audience with me early on in my writing career. I am thankful to you and wish you continued success in all your present and future endeavors.

To Debra McGregor of Cruise Planners. Thank you for being a major part of my focus group. You have always been one of the first to read my writings and give me feedback that assisted me in putting out great works. I appreciate you.

To Anthony Williams of Critickal Craft and Canvas.
I remember you telling me how profound my writings were and that I had a gift that would bring positive change globally. You have been a great friend and your words were very encouraging.

To Rendean Garrett, Founder of RenRising Talk Show. I have never met a soul as loving, genuine and giving as you. I remember clearly you getting emotional while interviewing me on your show after reading some of my writings. We developed a friendship that was very encouraging and loving. We will forever be connected spiritually. I love and miss you queen.

To Tera Roberson Stidum, Founder of She Dates Savvy. Thank you for taking time out to read my work and supporting my journey by sharing your positive energy. I appreciate you and much continued success. Keep your light shining.

To Kathy Sapp, Executive producer at Trifecta Entertainment/Tornante. You have also been a great influence to me in my writing career. Meeting you was a pleasure and I appreciate the support you have shown over the years. I'm sure we will meet again.

I would like to say thank you to everyone supporting my writing and dreams. I greatly appreciate you and God bless you.

Introduction

Much has been said about the relationship between the black woman and the black man. I understand that from our history the strength of our people and community has always manifested from the strength and unity of our families. Somewhere along the way some of us have started to believe the negative messaging that has been embedded in the minds of our people systemically and began to start living our family lives separately. We must counteract the destructive plan created by the evils of man and show undying love and support for each other all across this beautiful land.

Black women have always had the backs of black men and as a black man I will forever unapologetically display my love and respect for our beautiful black women endlessly.

The purpose of this book is to stimulate the mind, heart, body and soul of our black queens by writing very passionate and sensual poems of love reassuring them that they will forever have the respect, protection and affection of their strong black kings unconditionally for eternity.

Love Letters

A Love Letter to Our Beautiful Black Women

The Strength of Black Women

Yes I'm a queen
And the mother of all
Human beings
Take a stroll down your family tree
And I guarantee you will find a picture of
Me.

Many of our black kings
Were raped of their masculinity and thrust into
Slavery,
But I stood strong even in the absence of having the security
Of his arms being wrapped around
Me.

Our homes were broken
And multitudes of our children suffered a very traumatic
Price,
They were left to carry on without
Their fathers being a part of their
Lives.

Avery Washington

Without the protection of my king
I was raped repeatedly and stripped of what it felt like to be
Loved,
Damn you cowards for causing such a monstrous tragedy
Within our families who we
Beloved.

You seriously underestimated my loyalty to my family
And the undying love that I have for my
King.
I'm not only a queen, I'm a divine being
And I have the capabilities of achieving
Anything.

Through all of the pain you have caused
By your strategic plan of taking away the love of our
Black man
I now see a resurgence of love
With black women and men during my
Life span.

Many black men are now publicly speaking
And displaying their profound love for their
Black queens
Bringing back the strength and unity
That we once shared within the black
Community.

A Love Letter to Our Beautiful Black Women

I want every black man
In this world to clearly
Understand,
The heart and soul of a black woman
Needs the strength, protection and affection of the
Black man.

We need your love and loyalty
More than anything under
The sun.
We are your queens and you're our kings
And we need to protect our love by any means...
There is extraordinary power in the love between
The black man and black woman.

Avery Washington

Thank You

Thank you for believing in me,
Never leaving
Me
And trusting that our love
Would be for
Eternity.

Thank you for blessing me
With a beautiful
Family
I will forever be your rock
And be gentle when you need me to
Be.

Thank you for being patient with me
During the times I've let you
Down,
You've shown me unconditional love
By keeping me
Around.

A Love Letter to Our Beautiful Black Women

Thank you for allowing me
To learn how to love
You,
Others may have given up on me,
But you knew how to make my rough edges
Smooth.

There is no mistaken that you are
The woman of my
Dreams
Now the love we share is overflowing
Like a neverending
Stream.

It's because of you that I now make your heart smile brighter
Than anything under the
Sun.
There is no greater love to me than sharing the intimacy
Of being in a relationship with an intelligent and beautiful
Black woman.

Avery Washington

So in Love

I have never met a woman
Quite like
You
So sweet, sexy
And classy
Too.
You are a beautiful woman of great intelligence
And I'm so blessed to have you as my
Boo!
I'm so in love with you!

I know for sure
From this day
Forward
There is no other woman
Who I will adore
More.
You're the love
I've been searching
For.
I'm so in love with you.

A Love Letter to Our Beautiful Black Women

Heaven on Earth

Many people often wonder
If there is a place called
Heaven
Where our souls are filled with joy and laughter
And each day our lives are abundantly filled with
Blessings.

Heaven is usually a place
People visualize existing after our bodies depart from this
Earth,
Hoping that they will get to see this place
After doing God's
Work.

See I don't have to imagine
How heaven would
Be,
Because every night I have heaven
Resting in bed next to
Me.

Avery Washington

She is fearfully and wonderfully made
From her head down to her
Feet.
Connecting spiritually, mentally and physically
With a beautiful black queen is heaven to
Me.

A Love Letter to Our Beautiful Black Women

Your Sweet Nectar

Tonight I would like to celebrate
The love I have for
You
By preparing a special dessert in bed
That will taste delicious to me and pleasurable for
You.

Brace yourself for a tongue twisting experience
Filled with climactic oral
Sensations
The fire and desire that my body has for yours
Will fulfill your body with sensual and pulsating
Vibrations.

You are blindfolded
As I walk your chocolate, mocha, caramel body into the
Room.
You began to smell the seductive scent of your favorite candles
And it stimulates the very sexual woman inside of
You.

Avery Washington

I slowly kiss your lips
While removing your clothing and panties from your
Hips,
Gently lifting you in my arms
And placing your body into something
Wet and warm.

Softly biting your neck
While bathing your precious
Temple
My manhood has now become stimulated and I think it's time
For me to finish creating the erotic dessert that I can't wait to
Dive into.

I place your naked body
Onto the plate which is our
Bed,
Garnishing your body with strawberries and Champagne Toast,
Your favorite lotion and body spray as I widely open your
Legs.

A masterpiece has been created
And it's time for me to
Feast.
I'm ready to dive in head first
To taste you by penetrating my tongue inside of you
Deeply.

A Love Letter to Our Beautiful Black Women

Passionately tasting your sweet nectar
And caressing your cherry until your flower begins to
Cream,
Massaging your erogenous zone
While you have multiple orgasms and continue to
Scream.

There is no other woman on this earth
As beautiful as you and I will put that on
Everything.
I truly enjoyed tasting your love
And everything in
Between.

Avery Washington

Queen

She was such a vision of beauty
That I began to look for her
Wings.
Her eyes were dark brown
With the most radiant skin of melanin that I've ever
Seen.

Her intelligence outshines the intellect
Of all living
Things.
She is an angelical and impeccable
Black
Queen.

A Love Letter to Our Beautiful Black Women

Superwoman

Sometimes we complain
About some of the pettiest
Things
Like not having a pair of shoes
To wear with our favorite
Jeans

While many of our queens
Are fighting for their lives during summer, fall, winter
And spring
Not knowing if they will awake
To ever breathe
Again.

Lupus is a serious disease
Attacking many organs often causing flare-ups
And fatigue,
But I know of a woman
Who has a heart that no illness can
Defeat.

Avery Washington

She is a wife, mother, grandmother
And a very successful
Entrepreneur.
The essence of her soul
Will bless you abundantly and many can
Concur.

She inspires me and strengthens me,
Because I never saw her lose a
Fight.
She is a sister to me and a blessing to our family
And I love her dearly for
Life.

A Love Letter to Our Beautiful Black Women

Heart and Soul

Many people see vulnerability
In relationships as a sign of being
Weak,
But I see it as an opportunity for our hearts
To experience a deeper form of
Transparency.

Being completely open and honest in a relationship
Will leave no room for any type of
Deceit.
Allowing us to express our love on a deeper level
Where our souls began to
Speak.

A union based on principles
That are heavenly and not worldly is the
Key
To a healthier bond
That will last for
Eternity.

Avery Washington

Our love has a foundation
That is unbreakable and no other love can
Compete.
The love that we have is stronger than any other
And we are so blessed to have a love that is connected
Spiritually.

A Love Letter to Our Beautiful Black Women

Supposed to Be

Strength and independence
Like a gorgeous island in the middle of the
Sea,
Surviving the storms of this cruel world
While the winds blow away the leaves from the
Trees.

Taking on the whole world alone
With your grace
And beauty
While some men detach away from their roots and seeds,
Rolling away in the wind like
Tumbleweeds.

My goal as a family advocate
Is to continue to write words that speak of reality
And positivity
Implementing black love and unity
Back into our
Families.

Avery Washington

Our black women and children
Should never be left stranded alone in the middle of the
Sea.
I love you sincerely and will fight for you continuously,
Because this is not how our lives is
Supposed to be.

A Love Letter to Our Beautiful Black Women

Stimulating Conversations

There is nothing more sensual
Than a black woman stimulating my
Mental,
Your physical body is also beautiful,
But your intellect has my mind, body and soul wanting
You.

There is something sexual happening
When we gaze into each others
Eyes
As I provide encouraging words helping you spread your wings,
So that you will achieve all that you aspire to be as you fly
High above the skies.

To my mind and soul
Your words are
Invigorating
And the cadence of your voice
To my body is
Stimulating.

Avery Washington

No matter what we talk about
It leads to some type of
Penetration
The penetration of the mind, body and soul
Leading us to a night of passionate
Love making.

A Love Letter to Our Beautiful Black Women

Say Her Name

Something has been burning
Deep down inside of
Me
Like the crosses burned on the front lawns
Of people who look like
Me.

Strange fruit is what they called us
As they hung our bodies from
Trees
Leaving our blood dripping on the leaves
While cheering and laughing as they held hands with their
Families.

America says
That we are
Free,
But continue to enslave us
By employing slave catchers with the code name
Police.

Avery Washington

Arresting many of us
On bogus charges with so much blood on this
Land.
They are still hanging us in this present day.
Say her name
Queen Sandra Bland.

A Love Letter to Our Beautiful Black Women

Great Sacrifice

I remember when
You were pregnant with our very first
Child
And how you would get so emotional
Every once in a
While.

My undying love for you
Always found a way to make you
Smile,
Because there's nothing more loving
Than a woman sacrificing her life for the life of our
Child.

I realized that there would be times
When you would experience some fear
And anxiety,
But your love
Always brought out the best in
Me

Avery Washington

To provide everything
That you would need to put your heart at
Ease,
Like holding you tight through the night
So that you could sleep
Peacefully.

There were days
When you experienced many
Insecurities,
Wondering if you were going to get your body back
And if your stretch marks were going to last for
Eternity.

As we made love,
It was your body that I would passionately
Feast,
Slowly licking away all of your insecurities
And replacing your thoughts with love; making you feel secure
With me.

I will never take for granted
Your strength, intelligence
And beauty
I love and appreciate you for making great sacrifice
As you unselfishly risked your life to create our
Family.

A Love Letter to Our Beautiful Black Women

A Queen's Birthday

For fourteen thousand
And six hundred
Days
God has blessed upon this earth
A beautiful soul in the month of December on this nineteenth
Day.

Her outer beauty is flawless
And never cease to
Amaze,
But her inner beauty and accomplishments
As a woman is what I'd like to
Praise.

She has sacrificed her heart at times
To give love and support to others over the
Years.
I've witnessed the storms and the rain
The hurt and her pain, because I've been there to wipe away
Her tears.

Avery Washington

The funny thing about us
Is that everything we go through always happens in perfect
Time.
I have precisely been a part of her life
As she has been part of
Mine.

See there is an old cliche that says
Everything happens in God's
Time,
But many people use that as an excuse
And depend on others to lay down a ladder for them to
Climb,
But not my wife.

She has battled through the tough times
Of being a single mother at a young
Age,
Graduating from high school with her head held high
As she proudly walked across that
Stage.

Some people say life happens,
But I believe life happens if you let
It.
Kisha could have easily given up,
But she began to make conscious and strategic decisions about
Her life and will never regret it.

A Love Letter to Our Beautiful Black Women

She has spent over two decades in corporate America
While raising our three beautiful daughters at
Home,
Now she has taken a leap to help clients
Fulfill their vacation destinations with a travel agency of her
Very own.

My wife is a woman of great strength
Who made rough seasons bloom like the beautiful flowers of
Spring.
She also has a heart of gold
That has made the heart of every person in her life
Sing.

Kisha your soul has made a positive impact
On us all and people you don't even
Know.
As we honor you I want you to know that I truly love you
And you're the perfect role model for our three daughters to
Follow.

Avery Washington

Her Love

God I'm on my knees
Praying to you
Unselfishly
That someday you will bless me
With a beautiful black
Queen.

I will love and protect her
With all of my heart
Endlessly
And I vow to never disrespect or neglect her,
Because the love of her is valuable to
Me.

A Love Letter to Our Beautiful Black Women

King

If a man considers himself a King
His queen should never want for
Anything.
He should instinctively risk his life
To provide for his wife and their
Offspring.

In today's world the word king
Is thrown around very
Loosely.
When you meet a man
Make sure that he is
Worthy...
Worthy of your love.
Worthy of your touch.
Don't be afraid to say no
If what he has to offer you just ain't good
Enough.

Avery Washington

You are the greatest gift to man
And he should never strike you with his
Hands.
The penalty for any man
Abusing a woman as magnificent as you should be death
On your command.

The love of a black woman to me
Has a much deeper
Meaning,
Because the love I've received from black women
Has propelled me to overcome obstacles that God is still
Revealing.

I want you to understand that miracles larger than life
Is what the power of your love
Brings,
So the next time a man tells you he loves you
And presents you with a
Ring
Don't be afraid to say no
If his actions show that he is not fit to be your
King.

A Love Letter to Our Beautiful Black Women

If You Were Gone

If you were gone
Out of our lives
Forever
Black men would suffer a deep pain
That would go away
Never.

You have always been
The backbone of our
Communities.
If there were no you
There would be no
Me.

Without you we wouldn't
Have the strength to get through tough
Storms,
Because when we had fights with thunder and lightning
It was you who welcomed us with open
Arms.

Avery Washington

Too often you have been left to raise
Little black boys to become
Men
And that's a burden that no black man
Should ever thrust upon our precious black
Women.

I will never give up the fight
On advocating for the significance of your
Life
Until every black man understands
And takes a stand for all you have
Sacrificed.

A Love Letter to Our Beautiful Black Women

The Love of You

You gave me life,
So I must always protect your life with
Mine,
Never allowing anyone to disrespect beautiful black women
In or out of my
Bloodline.

A queen is what you are to me and eventually I will meet
A woman just as beautiful as
You.
On bended knee I will present her with a ring
And a love song is what our hearts will sing as she sheds tears
Saying I do.

A beautiful black family with little kings and queens
Is what we will be with a pet dog or
Two.
This joyous life I'm experiencing would never be
Wtihout the love of
You.

Avery Washington

Angel

You're an angel
Sent down from heaven
Above
Spreading your wings
Around my heart with your precious
Love.

There is nothing in this world
That I wouldn't do for
You,
Because during my tough times
Your love always brings me
Through.

I will always love you
Unconditionally for the rest of my
Life.
I thank God
For blessing me with you as my
Wife.

A Love Letter to Our Beautiful Black Women

The Rain

I never thought
That I would have opened my
Heart
To be so vulnerable for the love of someone
From the very
Start.

Your love was incredible
And we were
Inseperable
Your love was the master key
To my
Heart.

God has blessed me with more than
The precious love of
You
He also gifted me at the time
With the love of a beautiful baby girl
Too.

Avery Washington

A few years later I found myself on stage
In front of thousands of people on
Bended knee
Asking my beautiful black queen
To marry
Me.

Through love, laughter and pain
Our love has survived and is now thriving
Again.
We now have a family of three beautiful daughters
And I'm so glad that our marriage has survived the
Rain.

A Love Letter to Our Beautiful Black Women

Look In My Eyes

When you look into my eyes
I want you to clearly
See
That standing before you
Is a proud black man who loves you
Unconditionally.

I remember the times
We lay barefoot in the
Sands
Capturing precious memories of our love
On foreign
Land.

There was nothing foreign
About the language we spoke as we held each others
Hands,
The language we spoke was of love
Between a beautiful black woman and strong black
Man.

Avery Washington

When I look into your eyes
I can clearly
See
God has made me for you
And you were made for
Me.

A Love Letter to Our Beautiful Black Women

My Responsibility

There is a lot about your life
That goes
Untold
Like the numerous times you've put your dreams on hold
To help me achieve my
Goals.

As a man
I should have immediately taken a
Stand
By making great sacrifice to help you achieve your goals,
Because that is truly
God's plan.

There is no excuse for me
And I won't make
Any.
If I would have lived by God's plan
Our union would have been blessed
Abundantly.

Avery Washington

I deeply apologize for all the tears
Running through your
Eyes.
You are a beautiful queen deserving of all things
That make you smile deep down
Inside.

You are a strong woman
And you're not easily
Broken,
But me not being your king when you needed me to be
Has left you with a heart that will be hard for any good man to
Open.

Every night I pray for God to heal your heart
And bring to you a king that is
Worthy.
I'm a wiser man now and I truly want the best for you
I sincerely accept full
Responsibility.

A Love Letter to Our Beautiful Black Women

Tasty Love

Ooh how I love to kiss your precious flower
As I glide my fingers gently across your
Lips
Causing your heart to skip a beat
As you feel my tongue gain entrance inside of the lips between
Your hips.

Moisture is starting to set in
As I move the tip of my tongue throughout your
World.
Your muscles are starting to pulsate
While I gently use my lips to suck on your precious little
Pearl.

Your flower is now starting
To have uncontrollable
Contractions.
I'm the luckiest man alive
To be able to have a taste of your
Love and Satisfaction.

Avery Washington

The Proposal

I have been blessed with a beautiful queen
With the strength to conquer many
Things
Like continuing to win the battle over multiple sclerosis
While unselfishly making my heart
Sing.

For days at a time
Sometimes your body shuts
Down,
Just know that my undying love for you
Will never let you down and I will always be
Around.

You are such a blessing to me
And for your love I will do
Anything.
My heart and soul desires to be with yours
And to you I present this
Ring.

A Love Letter to Our Beautiful Black Women

A Deeper Connection

I have to pinch myself sometimes
To make sure that I'm not
Dreaming,
Just when we thought our love was over
God gave us both the inspiration to keep on
Believing.

Believing that our love
Would stand strong through the test of
Time,
Aging gracefully
Like the finest of
Wines.

We both caused each other heartache
And experienced so much
Pain.
I never thought that it would be possible
For us to embrace in each others arms
Again.

Avery Washington

Sometimes God will send us
Through storms under his
Protection,
So that we can establish a much deeper connection
Filled with
Love and affection.

A Love Letter to Our Beautiful Black Women

My Prayer

I have something
That I must express to
You.
Last night I prayed to God
That your heart would be renewed and to bless me with the love
Of you.

My soul was in need
Of another soul that was open to
Receive
The love from a man
That would transcend from the physical and love you for
Eternity.

When a man truly loves a woman
He will kneel and raise his
Hands
And ask God to transform him
From the material to a spiritual
Man.

Avery Washington

You are a beautiful queen
Deserving of all the gifts that royalty
Brings.
My love for you is everlasting
And I'm so blessed to be your
King.

A Love Letter to Our Beautiful Black Women

Loving You

Your love gave me the courage
To do the things that I wouldn't normally
Do
Like getting on one knee in front of thousands of people
The night I proposed to
You,
Like sacrificing my life
In the middle of the
Night
To protect the woman I love so much
And proudly call my
Wife.

Your love has always inspired me
To become a better
Man
Like listening to your heart's desires,
Because your wish is my
Command
Like kissing you on your forehead
Makes you feel comfortable and
Secure.

Avery Washington

My love for you has aged
Like the finest of wines and tastes so much better when its
Matured.

A Love Letter to Our Beautiful Black Women

Phone Sex

Every time I hear your voice
You send chills down my
Spine.
Flashbacks of making love to you
Immediately runs through my
Mind.

Your eyes hypnotize me
And your luscious body does
The Same.
I'm now in the mood to please you
With some sexual
Games.

I want you to remember how it feels
When I gently began to bite your inner
Thighs,
Slowly following behind with warm wet kisses
As you feel my tongue start to
Slide...

Avery Washington

I began to leisurely raise your skirt
To pull your panties to the
Side.
As soon as I get a glimpse of your love flower
My nature began to
Rise.

My mouth locks around your clit
And my thick tongue penetrates inside
Of you.
You grab the back of my head
Thrusting your pelvis as I
Please you.

Your body is squirming backwards
As if you were trying to run
Away.
You release your hands from around my head
And I lock my arms around your legs to make you
Stay.

I passionately moan as I go deeper and deeper
With every stroke of my tongue
Intimately.
Uncontrollably you scream as your body starts to cream
From the emotional sensations of my words entering you
Physically.

A Love Letter to Our Beautiful Black Women

Over and Over

If going through
All the things we've
Endured
Means that I will
Be with you for
Sure
And our love
Will last forever
More
I will do it over and over
And over
Again.

For you I will
Sacrifice my
Life,
Because of the joy
You bring me as my
Wife

Avery Washington

And for the love of you I will always
Fight
I will do it over and over
And over
Again.

I will continue to encourage you
To achieve all your passions
And dreams
By celebrating your accomplishments,
Because that is what a king does for his
Queen.
You are God's greatest creation
And capable of all
Things.
I will do it over and over
And over
Again.

A Love Letter to Our Beautiful Black Women

Hello

A simple hello to a stranger
Could be the very thing that saves someone's
Life.
Who would have thought
That my hello to you would lead to us being
Husband and wife?

The night we met it seemed
Like you were walking in slow
Motion.
Our eyes danced with each other
Without any words being
Spoken.

Butterflies ran through my stomach
And my heart began to beat very
Fast.
I was hypnotized by your beauty
And full of anxiety the first time we
Passed.

Avery Washington

Immediately and overwhelming
Calm came over
Me
As I approached to get to know you
A higher power took control of
Me.

Twenty years later and three beautiful kids
I'm still in love with the beautiful woman who has my heart
Forever gleaming.
Who would have thought
A word so simple like hello would hold such a profound
Meaning?

A Love Letter to Our Beautiful Black Women

Still in Love

Last night I sat outside
Of my favorite restaurant to
Write.
The love I felt inside my heart
Commanded me to call my wife for an
Invite,
Because I was missing her.

As I started writing intensively
I envisioned her here with
Me
And as I lifted my head to breathe
Approaching me was my beautiful
Queen
And I'm so glad she is here with me!

Our conversation was so engaging
And her alluring eyes were
Captavating.

Avery Washington

That night she had my heart rapidly pulsating
Giving me butterflies as if we had just started
Dating,
Because I'm still in love with her.

A Love Letter to Our Beautiful Black Women

A Precious Jewel

I'm so thankful
That God sent a woman so beautiful as you my
Way.
I'm very grateful
To have your love and companionship beaming through my soul
Everyday.

You are so lovely and bold
With a heart full of
Life.
Any man would be overjoyed
To have you as his
Wife.

To my life
You immediately added more value
Than I ever
Knew.
A precious jewel was gifted to me
More valuable than diamonds in the form of
You.

Avery Washington

You are more woman
Than any man could ever
Dream of.
I'm so blessed to have such a gorgeous lady in my life
Willing to trust me with all of her
Love.

A Love Letter to Our Beautiful Black Women

Making Sweet Love

I've never had a feeling
This strong
Before.
My mind is saying I'm moving too fast,
But my manhood is pulsating for
More.

More of the warm moist feeling
Of your love when I'm penetrating deep
Inside,
Feeling the opening and closing of your passion walls
As you repeatedly squeeze and relax your pelvic muscles while I
Take you for a ride.

You start to take control
By handcuffing me on my back to the
Bed,
Now I'm at your mercy as you mount me again
Hovering your phat vaginal lips on the tip of my thick shaft
Head.

Avery Washington

You slowly began to grind your clitoris against me
In a circular
Motion.
Stimulating every nerve in your body
As your flower gets wetter than an
Ocean.

Your heart is now beating fast
And you can now feel the pressure building
Up
So you place me inside of you
And began to ride me very
Rough.

You have positioned yourself
So that my love grinds your g-spot on every up and down
Slide
And every time I hit it
My nature gets harder and harder while you continue to
Ride.

We both are now moaning aggressively
And we are about to lose
Control.
I can feel your legs getting weak
And you are about to
Explode.

A Love Letter to Our Beautiful Black Women

Your volcano erupts
And at the same time I cum inside of
You.
Our bodies are shaking
From the multiple orgasms traveling through
You.

No matter what's going on in the world
It seems you know how to make my grey skies turn
Blue.
One of the greatest joys of life
Is making sweet love to
You.

Avery Washington

Your Smile

The last time we saw each other
We shared a passionate
Kiss.
The sun was shining so brightly
And our lives were filled with
Bliss.

I often dreamed that again someday
We would gaze into each others eyes for a
While.
To God I will continue to pray
For the day when I can again see you
Smile.

A Love Letter to Our Beautiful Black Women

Our Love Will Be...

We've had some
Good and bad
Times.
I would get on your nerves
And you would get on
Mine.

I used to think
That it would be just a matter of
Time
When you would go your way
And I would go
Mine.

People usually say
Things get better with
Time,
But when we decided to put God first
Everything else fell in
Line.

Avery Washington

Thankfully we both matured to see
Our relationship age
Gracefully
And now there is no doubt in our minds
That our love will be for
Eternity.

A Love Letter to Our Beautiful Black Women

Daily Motivation

You're my daily motivation
When I need to hear powerful words to stimulate
Me,
Because you're an intelligent and encouraging woman
Who truly understands just what I
Need.

The beauty inside of your heart is flawless
And your magnificent soul is filled with so much wisdom
And spirituality.
Often times I wonder
If I'm dreaming or living in
Reality.

Your love is like a light
Thats shines brighter and brighter
Everyday.
I thank God for the love of you
And every night I pray that our love will
Stay.

Avery Washington

I know deep down in my heart
That I have found a soul mate for
Life.
Thank you for feeding my spirit daily with everything I need
And I'm so blessed to have you as my
Wife.

A Love Letter to Our Beautiful Black Women

Not a Trophy to Me

I will never disrespect you
By marrying someone with blond hair and blue
Eyes.
I know you've been disappointed by some black men
Thinking that the slave master's daughter is some type of
Prize.

There is no other woman on this earth who is
Stronger and more beautiful than
You.
After all the torture this country has placed on your heart
You still continue to pull
Through.

America has always promoted white women
As the epitome of
Beauty
Now they're injecting their ass, lips and tanning their skin
Trying to achieve a body that looks like a beautiful black queen
Physically.

Avery Washington

As a black woman you are the embodiment of all
That is beautiful and that's
Evident.
As a black man I will marry you
And have beautiful princesses with your
Intelligence.

A Love Letter to Our Beautiful Black Women

The Vowel Renewal

Today is the day that I rededicate my life
To the most beautiful woman of my
Dreams.
You have made it possible for me
To experience just how good it feels to be in love with a
Queen.

I remember our first date as if it was yesterday
We argued the entire
Time.
Who would of thought twenty years later
That I would again be asking you to please be
Mine?

As I stand here before you and reflect on the unconditional love
You've given me throughout the
Years
My heart is beginning to feel heavy
And my eyes are swelling with
Tears.

Avery Washington

I admit there were times in our relationship
When I wasn't the best man I could
Be,
But there was something special about the love in your heart
That eventually brought out the best in
Me.

In my heart I knew that I truly loved you,
But to be honest it took me some time to learn how to show
You.
To show you love and appreciation for having you in my life
And passionately devoting all of me unconditionally to you
As my wife.

You totally turned my life around substantially
By blessing me with a magnificent
Family.
You will never have to worry about you without me,
Because we have decided on forever and that means
For eternity.

Kisha you are all I ever want and all I ever need.
You are the beautiful queen that makes my life
Complete.
After all we've been through we know that we are yoked equally.
I want you as my wife for the rest of my life, so will you please
Marry me?

I Love You

About the Author

Avery Washington is an American poet, family advocate and bestselling author. He was born in New Orleans, Louisiana and is one of the most respected authors of today. Avery is best known for advocating the significance of father and daughter relationships with his bestseller *Letters to My Daughters: Poetic Affirmations of Love from a Father.*

To learn more about Avery Washington visit:

http://averywashington.com (Website)
authoraverywashington (Instagram)

www.ingramcontent.com/pod-product-compliance
Lightning Source LLC
Chambersburg PA
CBHW020946090426
42736CB00010B/1292